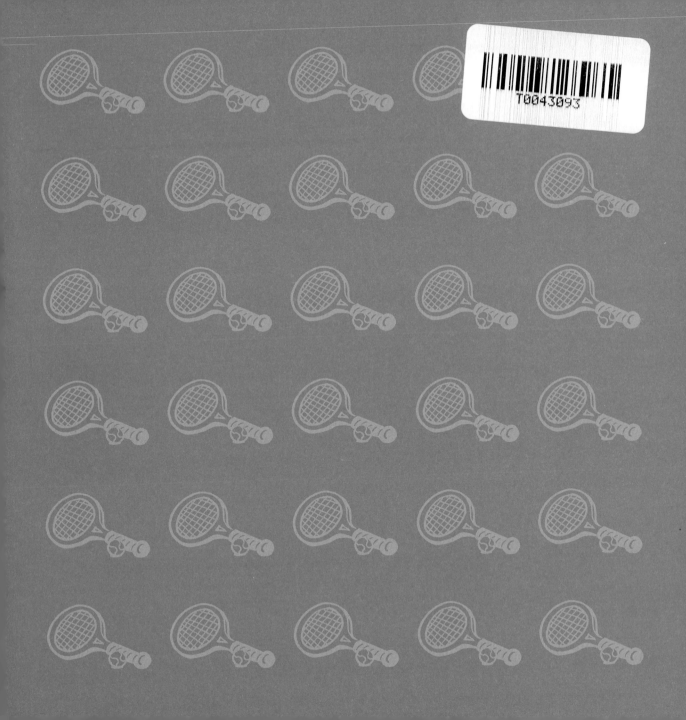

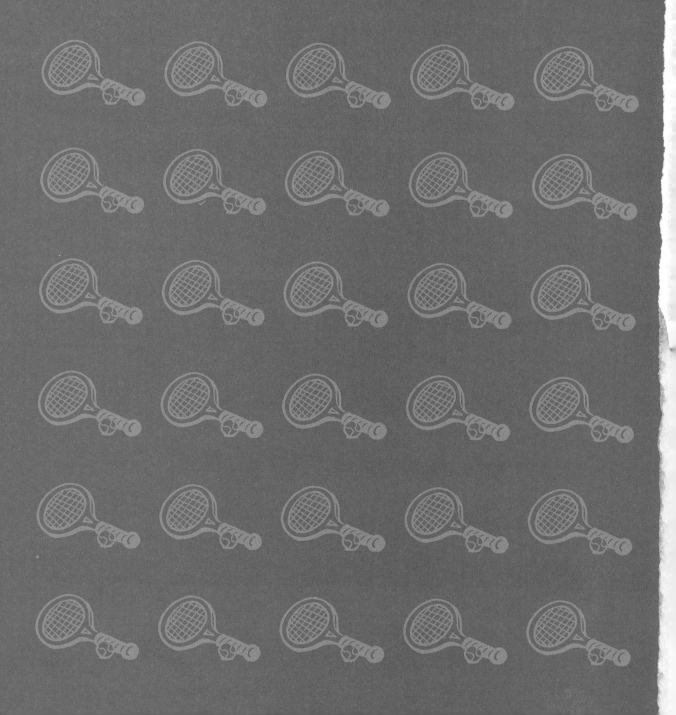

ORDINARY
PEOPLE
CHANGE
— THE —
WORLD

I am
Billie Jean King

BRAD MELTZER

illustrated by **Christopher Eliopoulos**

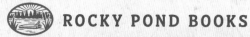 ROCKY POND BOOKS

I am **Billie Jean King.**

Fair play.

It's such a simple idea.

In sports and in life, it means you respect the rules and treat everyone equally.

But sometimes people don't want to play fair.

And other times, they don't even want to let you play.

But that never stopped me.

When I was little, people called me a tomboy, which is a word I still don't like.

Girls can enjoy sports just as much as boys.

Today, many dads encourage their daughters to play sports.
But back when I was growing up, my dad was one of the first.
Most important, he played equally with both me and my brother.
Equal time.
Equal respect.

NEVER UNDERESTIMATE YOUR OPPONENT.

YOU UNDERSTAND?

GOT IT.

NEVER UNDERESTIMATE YOUR OPPONENT, CHECK.

OUR DAD WAS A REALLY GOOD ATHLETE.

IN COLLEGE, HE USED TO PLAY AGAINST JACKIE ROBINSON.

I was so good at baseball, my dream was to be a professional player.
But when I went to my first real baseball game, I noticed something.

WHAT'S WRONG, BILLIE JEAN?

THERE ARE NO GIRLS ON THE TEAM.

ONLY BOYS.

It didn't seem fair.
I'd have to find another sport.

Fortunately, in fifth grade a friend asked me a question that changed my life.

My first time on the court, I had no idea what I was doing.

Back then, tennis was a game played mostly by wealthy people at fancy country clubs.

That wasn't my family. My mother sewed my white shorts; my racquet was borrowed.

A few weeks later, I heard about a coach named Clyde Walker, who gave free coaching on the public courts.
Often, the right teacher can change your life.

Coach Clyde taught me how to hold the racquet.
And he made tennis *fun*.

Now I just needed the right equipment.

To save money for a tennis racquet, I did odd jobs around the neighborhood, like taking out people's trash and weeding their gardens.

EVENTUALLY, I SAVED $8.29 IN A MASON JAR.

THAT'S ALMOST $75.00 TODAY.

ENOUGH FOR A RAQUET IN MY FAVORITE COLOR. PURPLE.

As a city employee, Coach Clyde traveled to a different park every day. My mom drove me for hours to get his free coaching, all across Long Beach, California.

WAIT.

YOU'RE THAT GIRL FROM YESTERDAY—AT THE OTHER PARK.

THAT'S ME.

THE ONLY WAY TO GET GOOD IS TO PLAY EVERY DAY.

SO WHAT'RE WE WORKING ON TODAY?

Mom didn't drive me because she thought I'd be rich.

Back then, playing tennis didn't pay much money, especially if you were a woman.

She drove me so I could do what I loved.

Not everyone cheered me on.
At one tournament, they wouldn't let me be in the group photo.

By the time I was twelve years old, at the fancy L.A. Tennis Club, I noticed something else: Everyone wore white . . . and everyone *was* white.

I wanted things to change.
Tennis shouldn't be a sport only for rich white people.
It should be a sport everyone can enjoy.

Every day, I worked with Coach Clyde.

I also worked at home.

My brother would practice pitching baseballs, and I'd make sure my tennis serves didn't knock over any lamps.

At fifteen, I had to write an essay about my future.

At sixteen, I started being coached by Alice Marble, a former number one tennis player who won eighteen Grand Slam championships, which are the biggest events of all.

THERE YOU GO, BILLIE JEAN...

SWING ALL THE WAY THROUGH.

She convinced me I could win—and made me realize how many strong women in sports had come before me.

I was part of something bigger than just myself.

Soon, a new thing also started happening.

BILLIE JEAN WINS!

BILLIE JEAN WINS!

With Coach Alice, I went from number nineteen in the country to number four.

By age seventeen, I made it all the way to Wimbledon.

We won the women's doubles title, which is when you play tennis with a partner.

We were the youngest team to ever do it.

BILLIE JEAN AND KAREN HANTZE WIN!

We couldn't afford to go to the big Wimbledon celebration ball.
But we enjoyed the victory.

As I started college, I was ranked number three in the country, but my school still didn't give me a scholarship.

SORRY, THERE ARE NO SCHOLARSHIPS FOR GIRLS.

WAIT A MINUTE.

I'M ONE OF THE LOWEST RANKED PEOPLE ON THE TENNIS TEAM, AND *I* HAVE A FULL SCHOLARSHIP.

SHE'S THE BEST PLAYER ON CAMPUS AND ONE OF THE BEST IN THE WORLD, AND SHE GETS *NOTHING*?

THAT'S NOT FAIR.

THIS IS LARRY.

HE ALWAYS WANTED MEN AND WOMEN TO BE TREATED EQUALLY.

I MARRIED HIM A FEW YEARS LATER.

Over the years, even as my career moved forward, people still didn't treat women equally.

When a man won a tournament, he'd get a big check.

When a woman won the same tournament, she was paid much less.

When a man won, the reporters would ask him questions about the match.

When a woman won, they'd ask...

People would tell me that's just how the world worked.

Women were paid less than men.

They were treated worse than men.

I knew I had to change it.

Soon, I achieved one of the greatest victories of my career.

CONGRATULATIONS, BILLIE JEAN!

YOU WON THE BIG ONE— THE SINGLES TITLE AT WIMBLEDON!

After winning Wimbledon a second time—in singles, doubles, and mixed doubles (which is when men and women play together)—I thought things would get better for women.

They didn't.

IN 1968, THE MAN WHO WON WIMBLEDON GOT $4,800.

I WON FOR A THIRD STRAIGHT YEAR AND GOT $3,000 LESS.

AND IT WASN'T JUST ME.

WOMEN WERE PAID LESS THAN MEN IN ALMOST EVERY JOB.

There were so many tennis greats who came before me—

SUZANNE LENGLEN

MAUREEN CONNOLLY

ALTHEA GIBSON

ALICE MARBLE

HELEN WILLS MOODY

Each of them taught me something. It's like they were there with me, on one team.

THAT'S HOW IT IS, LADY.

FANS BUY TICKETS TO SEE MEN, NOT WOMEN.

I was the number one player in the world, but I was being paid so little, I couldn't even get a credit card. It was time to take action.

When tournaments didn't offer equal pay, we started protesting.

They called us The Original Nine.
Thanks to our women's tour, tournament organizers quickly realized fans would pay just as much to see us play.

Soon after, I was the first woman ever named *Sports Illustrated*'s Sportsperson of the Year.

But with every step forward, there was always someone who wanted to move things back.

His name was Bobby Riggs.

At one point in time, he was the number one tennis player in the world.

Now he was fifty-five years old and a loudmouthed bully.

Bobby Riggs insisted women weren't as strong as men.

To prove it, he challenged me to a match. When I refused, he challenged Margaret Court, who had recently become the number one female player in the world.

BOBBY RIGGS WINS BOTH SETS! 6-2 AND 6-1!

I heard the score in an airport. My reaction was instantaneous.

I WANT TO PLAY HIM.

It was called the Battle of the Sexes, the biggest tennis match the world had ever seen. I knew what was at stake. Bobby treated it like it'd be easy.

YOU SHOULD TRAIN.

BILLIE JEAN IS REALLY GOOD.

MARGARET WAS #1, AND I BEAT HER.

BILLIE JEAN WILL BE EASY TOO.

SHE'S JUST A GIRL.

The match was set at the Astrodome, a massive stadium in Texas.

Since it had a white roof, I knew it would be hard to see the tennis ball when it was up high in the lights.

I also knew Bobby liked to hit them high, so for weeks, I practiced hitting 150 overhead shots *every single day.*

YOU SURE YOU KNOW WHAT YOU'RE DOING?

YUP.

HIT ME ANOTHER HIGH ONE.

Instead of playing best of three, which was what women usually played, we decided to play best of five.

BOBBY SAID WOMEN COULDN'T HANDLE LONGER MATCHES.

I NEED TO SHOW PEOPLE HE'S WRONG.

YOU SURE YOU KNOW WHAT YOU'RE DOING?

YUP.

HIT ME ANOTHER ONE.

The prize money was a record-setting $100,000, winner take all.

Around this time, I also realized I was gay.

Being gay means that if you're a girl, you love and have romantic feelings for other girls—and if you're a boy, you love and have romantic feelings for other boys.

If I lost the match, I knew it would erase everything I'd achieved in tennis.

But I was ready to win.

In fact, the night before, I called my brother and told him to place a bet.

On the big day, I went over my game plan and did the most important thing of all:

I read through the hundreds of letters that had come that week from fans.

This wasn't just a tennis match.

It was a fight to prove how strong women were.

Little girls around the country were counting on me.

On September 20, 1973, 30,000 fans packed the Astrodome. Ninety million more were watching on TV, which is more than some Super Bowls.

To this day, it is the most watched tennis match *ever*.

This was the big time.
The world was watching.
Now I just had to deliver
the right statement.

At the beginning of the match, Bobby was wearing a jacket.
He was slower than I thought he'd be.

I didn't hold back.

When I went up a few points, he took off his jacket.
It didn't help.

Of course, he tried hitting them up high. I was ready.

As the match went on, I didn't miss a single overhead shot. Just like I practiced.

Bobby wasn't talking or bragging anymore. He was scared, breathing heavily.

He was just another bully. And every bully can be defeated.

BILLIE JEAN KING WINS!

BILLIE JEAN KING WINS!

SHE WON!

BILLIE JEAN KING WINS!

THE WOMAN WON.

BILLIE JEAN KING WINS!

THE WOMEN WIN.

I crushed him in three straight sets: 6–4, 6–3, 6–3.
He didn't win a single one.

BILLIE JEAN KING WINS!

WE WON!

For millions, it was the very first time they'd seen a woman beat a man at anything.

Riggs jumped over the net to congratulate me.

The first words he said were . . .

I UNDERESTIMATED YOU.

He did.

After my victory, I testified before Congress on the Education Equality Act, which would fund the goals of Title IX and make sure that girls' sports got the same amount of money as boys' sports.

In my life, people expected me to dress like a girl.
Act like a girl.
And hit like one.
I did.
I *always* hit the ball like a girl, which means harder
and more powerfully than anyone.

All of us are powerful in our own ways.
So how do you get to be your best self?
By practicing, sweating, and giving everything you've got.
And when you have nothing left, give more.

Playing fair is the same in both sports and life.
If everyone doesn't get the same chance, you'll
never find out who's truly the best.
Real victory doesn't come from points scored.
It comes from how you treat others in the game.
No one really wins until everyone gets to play.

I am Billie Jean King, and I champion equality.

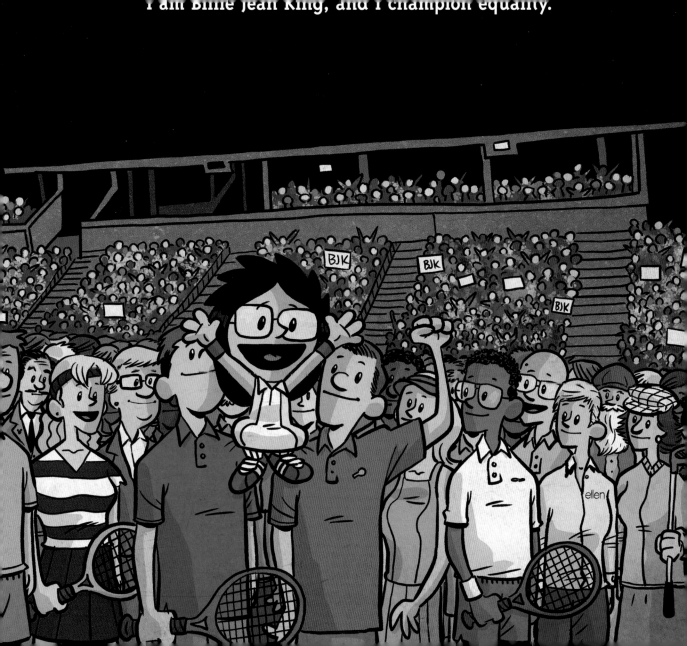

"Be bold. If you're going to make an error, make a doozy, and don't be afraid to hit the ball."
—**Billie Jean King**

Timeline

NOVEMBER 22, 1943	1961–1964	1961	SEPTEMBER 17, 1965	1966	1966, 1967, 1968, 1971, 1972, 1974
Born in Long Beach, California	Attends California State University	Wins first doubles title at Wimbledon	Marries Larry King	Wins first singles title at Wimbledon	Is ranked number one in women's tennis

Billie Jean with
her father

Billie Jean as Grand Marshall
of the NYC Pride Parade, 2018

Billie Jean and Bobby Riggs
before the Battle of the Sexes

Winning Wimbledon
in 1972

Billie Jean and her
partner, Ilana Kloss

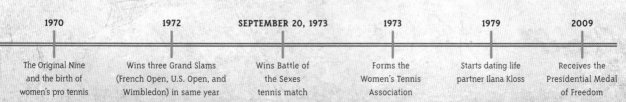

1970	1972	SEPTEMBER 20, 1973	1973	1979	2009
The Original Nine and the birth of women's pro tennis	Wins three Grand Slams (French Open, U.S. Open, and Wimbledon) in same year	Wins Battle of the Sexes tennis match	Forms the Women's Tennis Association	Starts dating life partner Ilana Kloss	Receives the Presidential Medal of Freedom

For my Aunt Debbie,
one of my favorite sports fans,
as well as our other LGBTQ friends and family,
whom we love and support
for being exactly who they are
—B.M.

For Elizabeth, Alexa, Megan, Christopher, and Jennifer Rand.
They make my life more fun!
—C.E.

For historical accuracy, we used Billie Jean King's actual dialogue whenever possible. For more of Ms. King's true voice, we recommend and acknowledge the below titles. Special thanks to the inspiring and amazing Billie Jean King—as well as the generous Tip Nunn—for their input on early drafts (and for all the photo references too).

· ·

SOURCES
Autobiography of Billie Jean King by Billie Jean King (HarperCollins, 1982)

Billie Jean by Billie Jean King with Frank Deford (Viking, 1982)

Pressure Is a Privilege by Billie Jean King with Christine Brennan (LifeTime Media, Inc., 2008)

Game, Set, Match: Billie Jean King and the Revolution in Women's Sports by Susan Ware (UNC Press, 2011)

PBS American Masters documentary, 2013: http://www.pbs.org/wnet/americanmasters/billie-jean-king-film-billie-jean-king/2637/

Publisher's Letter by Billie Jean King, *womenSports* magazine, August 1977

FURTHER READING FOR KIDS
Good Night Stories for Rebel Girls 2 by Elena Favilli and Francesca Cavallo (Timbuktu Labs, 2018)

Women in Sports: 50 Fearless Athletes Who Played to Win by Rachel Ignotofsky (Ten Speed Press, 2017)

· ·

ROCKY POND BOOKS • An imprint of Penguin Random House LLC, New York

First published in the United States of America by Dial Books for Young Readers, an imprint of Penguin Random House LLC, 2019
This edition published by Rocky Pond Books, an imprint of Penguin Random House LLC, 2023

Text copyright © 2019 by Forty-four Steps, Inc. • Illustrations copyright © 2019 by Christopher Eliopoulos

Portrait of Billie Jean King (page 38) and photo of Billie Jean with Bobby Riggs (page 39) courtesy of Bettman/Getty Images. Photo of Billie Jean with her father (page 39) courtesy of Billie Jean King. Photo of the NYC Pride Parade (page 39) courtesy of Steven Ferdman/Stringer/Getty Images. Photo at Wimbledon (page 39) courtesy of Evening Standard/Stringer/Getty Images. Photo of Billie Jean with Ilana Kloss (page 39) courtesy of Michael Tran/Getty Images.

Visit us online at PenguinRandomHouse.com.

Library of Congress Cataloging-in-Publication Data
Names: Meltzer, Brad, author. | Eliopoulos, Chris, illustrator. • Title: I am Billie Jean King / by Brad Meltzer ; illustrated by Christopher Eliopoulos. | Description: New York : Dial Books for Young Readers, an imprint of Penguin Random House, LLC [2019] | Series: Ordinary People Change the World | Audience: Ages: 5–8. | Audience: Grades: K to Grade 3. | Identifiers: LCCN 2018031285 | ISBN 9780735228740 (hardcover) | Subjects: LCSH: King, Billie Jean—Juvenile literature. | Women tennis players—United States—Biography—Juvenile literature. | Tennis players—United States—Biography—Juvenile literature. • Classification: LCC GV994.K56 M45 2019 | DDC 796.342092 [B]—dc23 LC record available at https://lccn.loc.gov/2018031285

ISBN 9780735228740 • 10 9 8 7 6 5 4

Manufactured in China • Designed by Jason Henr • Text set in Triplex • The artwork for this book was created digitally.